THE SOUL OF A BLACK WOMAN:

Journeys Through Poetry

Meika J Cole

Copyright © 2017 Meika J Cole

ISBN-13: 978-1537721002
ISBN-10: 1537721003

All rights reserved. This book is protected under the copyright laws of the United States of America. No part of this publication may be reproduced, distributed, or transmitted in any form or by any means, including photocopying, recording, or other electronic or mechanical methods without the written permission of the publisher except for brief quotations embodied in critical reviews.

THE SOUL OF A BLACK WOMAN:
JOURNEYS THROUGH POETRY
by Meika J. Cole
Published by Jaye-Simone Publishing
Bloomfield Hills, MI 48301

Scripture quotations are taken from the Amplified® Bible (AMPC), Copyright © 2015 by The Lockman Foundation Used by permission. www.Lockman.org.

Cover Design: Meika Cole & Canva.com

DEDICATION

I dedicate this book to every woman who has stood before me granting me the freedom to express myself while on this journey called life. To my beautiful daughter, Laila Jaye-Simone, I do this for you so that you may begin to recognize the power that resides within. Don't you ever forget it. Don't let anyone try to take your power from you.

CONTENTS

Acknowledgements
Introduction   1

Part I: The Soul of a Black Woman   13
Journey Prayer #1   14
Black Woman   19
Who They Say I am   21
Still, I Struggle   23
Journey Prayer #2   27
Tired   29
Secrets   31
4 a.m. Questions   33
Spiritual Warfare   36
Alone   38
Real Life   42
Conversation with Different Gods   43

Part II: Dark Places   48
Journey Prayer #3   49
Heart Realities   55
To Have and to Hold   57
Lying to Myself   59
I Cheated   61
En Route Thoughts   63
What You Doing Girl   67
Lost Dreams   71
Baby Momma   75
Side Chick Confessions   78
Dear (Insert Name)   82

Friend Zone   84
Scared   85
Journey Prayer #4   87

Part III: Welcome Back to the Light   90

Journey Prayer #5   95
Freedom   97
Hey, Did I Ever Apologize   99
I AM the Prize   102
Revelations   104
Kinda Love   106
A Better View of Him   110
Just One Time   112
Worthy   114
Renewed   115
All is Well   117
For Laila   118

About the Author

ACKNOWLEDGEMENTS

This book is dedicated to my mom and dad, Dorothy and Al J. Cole. Dad, although you are not here physically, your spirit still lives on. I have never abandoned the pride that you had in me to do things better. Mom, you raised some ambitious women and I thank you for always guiding me when I needed it, supporting my dreams, drying up the tears, cleaning up my mess, and giving me a good dose of reality when I locked myself away in my own protective bubble.

To my sister Anetria (Nay) Cole, you were my motivator and you never allowed me to give up even when I wanted to. Thanks for helping me resurrect my voice and for being the example I needed to move towards my dream.

To the Byas, Cole, Green, Jones, Kaiser-Lee, and Tademy families, thank you for your unconditional love and support. Alice, Cicely, Daveda, Jonice, India, LaKisha, Marita, Shaina,

Shannon and Tammy, thanks for believing in my gift and pushing me when I was not sure if my voice was really my voice. Thinking back on the good, bad, and indifferent days, you guys always held me down and encouraged me to do what God birthed me to do.

To my crew, Arthur (man, you came into my life at the right time), Bobby, Cedric (Shantele), Corey (LaWanda), Juan (Littisha), Khary, Mandell (Jackie), and Orian, thanks for being a listening ear and the male balance that I needed to pump this thing on out. To the wives, thanks for making them the men they are.

To Pastor Leon, Lady Kalonda and the Winners Circle Church family in Oakland and Macomb counties, thanks for the foundation in applying God's word in my life.

To my heartbeat, my mini-me, the joy of my life, Laila. I thank God so much for presenting you to me. You have helped me grow into a finer woman and mother. You encourage me to go hard or go home. I do this all for you and I pray that I spark the flame in you early on to be confident in who the Creator made you to be.

To every woman reading this, I urge you to share your testimonies and help someone else along the way. When I think about the dark places I had grown accustomed to, I had to force myself to remember that even there, I still had to find my light. When you've experienced disappointment after disappointment and through it all you keep on, that is the greatest testament to God that you still got fight in you, simply because you remembered that you had a light beneath all of that. I am so glad I don't look like what I have experienced.

INTRODUCTION

The art of just **"being"** is easy, but **"being" "black"** and a **"woman"** in a world that criticizes you for being are all three, is a continuous battle that we will fight until the end of time

Meika J Cole

What is the Soul of a Black woman and what makes it different from the souls of any other woman? The soul is defined as "the moral and emotional nature of human beings." While each woman has her own characterization of what makes up her existence, the soul of a Black woman has innate roots that were conceived out of struggle and triumph. It encompasses the pain that we have endured, and it shapes our perception of perseverance and individual development.

What makes the journey different is the reality of what Black women lost along the way. Every aspect of our character was purchased at a price--and that price was the embezzlement of our identity. Despite it all, we still have overcome. Black women have beat the odds. The art of just **"being"** is easy, but **"being"** **"black"** and a **"woman"** in a world that criticizes you for being all three, is a continuous battle that we will fight until the end of time.

THE SOUL OF A BLACK WOMAN

Being a Black woman in America, is by far, one of the greatest challenges that I have had to endure. In one instance, I'm fighting to construct my place in the world, but then on the other hand, I question if where I have set up residence is where my spirit is supposed to rest. Being a Black woman has shown me my strengths, my weaknesses, and all the in between.

I will admit, I battled with myself for some time about releasing this work. I didn't know if I wanted to expose myself or the situations of other sisters who some of these poems were inspired by. However, I felt it was my duty to vocalize these emotions. As women, we are in the constant battle of "*us*" versus "*them*". Either we are fighting against the constructed ideologies of what it means to be a Black woman in a White America, or we are laboring to defend ourselves within our own African-American collective. Being a Black woman is enough stress within itself, but when you add titles like Christian, daughter, sister, friend, mother, employee, and wife (to name a few), the plight seems to intensify. Because Black women are considered as the pillars of their collective, it is believed that we are inclined to struggle because that is what Black women before us did, and they made due.

The concept of being a Strong, Black Woman puts so much pressure on us, which conditions us to believe that life gets no better and struggle is what we do best. We allow ourselves to be passive, minimizing our needs, nevertheless placing the needs of others over our own. We have husbands to please, employers to serve, children to nurture, and parents to care for—yet forgetting that somewhere along the way, we must take care of ourselves.

Oh, and please, don't get me started on the concept of being "**Single**", "**Black**" and a "**Woman**". In a world that circumscribes an individual to a relationship status, singleness is not a title that most Black women want to carry. Depending on who you are debating with, a clear majority of people still believe that the most important job of a woman is to bear children and become a wife. Honestly, you too may feel the same way, but the world just isn't set up like that anymore. There are various factors which makes that patriarchal dream seem less ideal, especially if you are a Black woman.

In comparison to other minorities, relationships are argued to be extremely problematic for Blacks, specifically the ideology which argues that most Black men don't want to commit. From music to television, everything that's being marketed to us always highlights a Black man's inability to remain faithful or even commit to any kind of relationship with Black women. Then there are other factors such as the increase in down-low brothers, and the high imprisonment rates of Black males, which creates an unbalanced ratio of us to them.

I could be wrong, but I do believe that no one *really* wants to be alone. As a single woman myself, I feel your pain. You are often bombarded with a bunch of asinine questions like: "Why are you still single?" "Do you think that your standards are unrealistic?" "Do you ever get lonely?" "Do you think that you will ever get married?" "Have you tried online dating?" Girl, the list goes on. I mean really, let's be honest, doesn't it get irritating at times? I mean come on, it's cool when you are just getting out of a relationship or if you aren't ready to settle down, but when the heart transitions into the "I'm ready to move on" stage, some people lose patience as they wait for the right opportunity to present itself. Amid it all, being the emotional creatures that we are, we often find ourselves in relationships that were never intended for us, thus leading us right back where we started-- Confused and rejected.

    Another concept that burns my soul is the theory of Dating While Black. What does that mean you ask? It means that brothers often contend that because you are single, Black and a woman, there must be something in your DNA that prevents you from being who they want you to be. Oh, please, don't even let me venture into the discourse of submission, because some of them argue that as Black women, we are not willing to submit either. So now, not only am I cursed for being a single, Black Woman, now, I don't even know my role as one either.

Now what happens? Black women find themselves questioning their worth. Then you end up asking yourself some questions like, "What's wrong with me?" "Am I pretty enough?" "Will I ever find a man that will genuinely love me for me?" Am I light enough? Should I bleach my hair blonde, or should I buy 24" bundles instead?" Sisters, that is exactly what I am doing with this book. I am vocalizing what you feel internally but may not want to admit. I talk about the highs and lows. The engagements, births, divorces and the "I don't know" moments. The journey that I am about to take you on is a collection of thoughts, raw emotion, and situations that myself and other women have experienced. My journey has not been a cakewalk **WHATSOEVER**.

Just like you, I've had to overcome some hurdles: I was victimized as a child, which gave me trust problems. I lost my father at twelve, so I suffer from daddy issues. I was raised by a hardworking, single mother, so I'm used to being in control of my household. I didn't particularly belong to any crowd. I have searched for love in **ALL** the wrong places. I have been naïve. Love almost costed me my freedom. I've witnessed sorrow from people who I regarded as my friends. I've been lied on, mistreated, and passed over more times than I care to admit. I've had to overcome challenges in the workplace. I wasn't polished enough. Not Black enough. Because I advocate for African-American lives, I have been called a racist. I struggle with my weight. I've been bankrupt emotionally and financially. I have battled depression, lost children, and struggled hard as a single parent.

Although there is pain behind the masks that we all put on, I have found that we all have rich stories, but sharing them becomes problematic because we are so concerned about what other people will think. Nonetheless, that is when I got a "But God" epiphany down on the inside. I had to look to the hills to where my help came from and I had to learn how to speak life into my being. I am beautiful. I am smart. I am the head and not the tail. I am the apple of God's eye. I am being refined and will come out as pure gold. I am the prize and not an option.

I had to learn that I had a divine purpose that was meant for me, specifically, and no one could do my work but me. Sometimes your struggle isn't for you alone. You must go through to be able to give God the glory to help others overcome theirs as well. Down in my heart, I believe God does, in fact, allow us to be tested to bless others when they are going through.

See, I am just as human as you are. Sometimes I cuss, I cry, and I may even have a drink all while asking God for his forgiveness, direction, and intervention (NO, SERIOUSLY). **I DO NOT, UNDER ANY CIRCUMSTANCES,** have it all together (and neither do you), which is why I know for certain that we all need God to be with us. It's called balance. I am just a soul and I fall short of His glory daily, but that failure doesn't negate the fact that I know that there is a foundation. I am not overly "churchy" nor am I too "worldly". I am just a woman who trusts God to use me, even in my residence of despair.

The Soul of a Black Woman: Journeys Through Poetry, serves as an ethnographic account of the emotions that myself and other women have had to overcome on their journey. I get inspiration from reading and conversing with other women about their struggles. Using narratives, I capture some of these moments, while offering balance through God's word. You may laugh, cry, or may get upset as you revisit those moments, but trust me, it's all about healing. Heck, none of this may even correspond to your struggles and that's fine, but it may be just the thing that someone else you know may need to hear. Our struggles are what they are, but just know that they are the building blocks needed to stabilize your foundation, while you venture this thing we call life.

MEIKA J COLE

PART I: THE SOUL OF A BLACK WOMAN

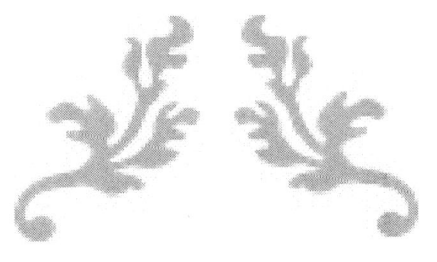

"Sometimes you just must make your mistakes, chalk it up, and tie it to your heart. Next, you tuck them away in the life experiences vault, and act normal because as a Black woman, you are expected to. If you don't you are deemed weak"

Meika J Cole

JOURNEY PRAYER #1

Father God, I come to you asking you for help God. Lord, I struggle because while I know that you created me for a purpose, I often get so lost in life. Lord, I don't understand my journey. I need you to show me that I am indeed worthy. Jehovah God, humble me and reveal my faults. Lord, lift me up and allow me to move past the lies that the Enemy has tried to tell me about who I am. Lord, help me to be content with who I am. Lord, help me to love the skin I am in and allow me to stand against anyone who may question my role as a Black woman. Lord, your word says:

"And do not be conformed to this world [any longer with its superficial values and customs], but be transformed *and* progressively

changed [as you mature spiritually] by the renewing of your mind [focusing on godly values and ethical attitudes], so that you may prove [for yourselves] what the will of God is, that which is good and acceptable and perfect [in His plan and purpose for you]."

Romans 12:2

Help me to believe and see the power that you birthed in me.

In Jesus Name, Amen

As Black women, we have conditioned ourselves to become overly consumed by what the world says we should and shouldn't be. Now before you get to slapping fives and snapping fingers, I need you to get into your quiet place, clear your mind, and reflect for a minute. I must ask you, just who are you, sister? What is your reason for being here? The word states:

"Upon You have I relied and been sustained from my birth; You are He who took me from my mother's womb and You have been my benefactor from that day. My praise is continually of You."

Psalms 71:6 AMP

That declaration right there solidifies just what the Father knows about you. It demonstrates the confidence that we should have in believing that who He created, is indeed someone who is special and worthy of every good thing created in the Earth realm. So why do you question it?

This section took a lot out of me because I recall being right in that moment in my life where I knew, but wasn't too sure. I mean, I was a mother, daughter, sister, friend, college graduate, college student, caseworker, soon-to-be author etc. But honestly, excluding the fancy titles, I was just a Black woman trying to find her way.

You can be the most beautiful, financially set woman in the world and still lack confidence in your ability. I think that once we begin taking pride in our gifts and truly learning thyself, we take some of the stress away, thus allowing ourselves to just, be. Sometimes you just have to make your mistakes, chalk it up, and tie it to your heart. Next, you tuck them away in the life experiences vault, and act normal because as a

Black woman, you are expected to. If you don't you are deemed "weak", but don't adhere to that fallacy because God does in fact have a divine plan and purpose for you. Don't let the Devil keep you in a place of inferiority.

BLACK WOMAN

Your soul ascends beyond what is imaginable,
A strength so profound, that others try and duplicate you.
From the size of your lips,
To the curve in your hips,
Added with your other spiritual gifts
Black Woman,
you are the prototype.
You possess strength and femininity,
Adorned in God's image of perfection
and divinity.
Black woman
Remember the grace and assignment placed on your life, your title extends far beyond mother or wife. You are a vessel.
In God's eyes, you are special
and he molded you with abilities

that you ain't even tapped into.
Stop losing yourself when the world criticizes you. Mocking your Afrocentric style all while monetizing the image of you.
Black woman,
when will you stop allowing others to define you?

WHO THEY SAY I AM

They say that
I'm a mother
A teacher
Student
and his fantasy.
I'm a welcome Mat
Problem solver
and a personal assistant
Yep, that's me!!
I'm conceited and materialistic.
I'm fierce and flawless
I'm confrontational
I don't know my position
and I am lower in the hierarchy.
I give life lessons to my sons
I prime daughters to be mothers
but they don't realize that

I'm often alone
Bearing my insecurities,
My fears and the rejections
But eventually I shake it off.
When you are a Black Woman,
There's no backing down.
Being Strong is in my DNA
It's never ok to let them see you sweat
cuz' you are a Black Woman,
You must carry all of that.
That's what they think I am.

STILL I STRUGGLE

Here I am, cognizant of the powers that I
possess within,
But then again, I struggle.
I struggle with the fact that by birthright
I'm held to a higher degree.
I struggle as many contemplate,
What they think my role as a woman supposed
to be.
Generations of Black women ran,
risking their lives just to be free,
detaching me from the bondage
of their painful history.
So, I gotta hold steadfast to that strength,
because Mama said it's embedded in me.
I struggle with my name
cuz' it ain't as simple as Bethany,
so regardless of my education and title,

the recruiters straight look over me.
I struggle with the tone of my voice
and the confidence that I have within,
now I minimize my identity
just so I don't offend.
If I perm my hair,
I'm not Black enough,
but If I rock afros and dreads
I'm too pro black, and stuff.
So, I sit right here trying to be content with the middle.
I struggle with the fact that when I turn on the TV, there's no true representation of me.
See, I'm supposed to be
Versed like Angela Davis
Yet ride or die Like Assata.
In between all of this,
I'm supposed to cook just like my grand momma,
not to mention,
be intelligent and poised as Michelle Obama?

My brothers want me flawless like those
models they see on TV
So, I spend hours in the gym or under a knife
Getting my body right
in hopes that someday he will make me his
wife.
I am supposed to train up my babies into ladies
and sons into men
While hiding the real struggle
That I bear within.
I'm supposed to act docile and smile
When oppression overtakes my community,
Crying as they turn future prophets
into dead bodies.
I'm supposed to fight the good fight
Praying that everyone gets it right.
I'm not supposed to be angry
Cuz' they say that ain't what a Psalms 31
woman should be.
So, I load up my emotions
And smile like I'm content

Lord, this can't be the kind of life you meant for me.

JOURNEY PRAYER #2

Jehovah Heavenly Father, I come to you in prayer with a heavy heart. God, your word says, **"For I know the plans and thoughts that I have for you,' says the Lord. 'Plans for peace and well-being and not for disaster to give you a future and a hope." Jeremiah 29:11 AMP**

But God, sometimes I ask, where are you? Is this really the plan you had for MY life? Why so much despair? Why did you make me a Black woman when you already knew that the odds would be stacked against me? I struggle in my relationships, I struggle in knowing myself. Honestly, I struggle with trusting YOU. Why does the world seem so against me? Why do I have to fight so hard to fit in? Why do I have to go through so much? Life just isn't easy for me. Lord, show me. Guide me. Help me change my questions. Lord, give me answers. Lord, what is the lesson in all of this? God, help me to be better at accepting it, although I may not understand the "why." I trust that you will make things clearer for me. Please Father, my patience is getting thin.

In Jesus Name,
Amen.

TIRED

I grow tired of praying,
hoping,
and being patient.
My soul fights daily to keep going,
even though I may feel like it isn't worth it.
I get tired of being told to just be strong.
Sometimes I need you to just listen
Try to understand that there's a lot going on within me.
My spirit is crushed when I am unable to see
my progress,
well after getting the degree,
working the job
waiting to be promoted,
chosen
and appreciated.
I get tired of being teased with opportunities,

leading to more
disappointment,
insecurity,
and despair.
But then again, really, why should I care?
Although it hurts,
it's the reality that I must bear.

SECRETS

The despoliation of her innocence
Made her set up distance in her heart
Revisiting the moment
when her world was torn apart.
In one instance
her destiny was aligned with shame,
because a man defiled her
who shared the same last name.
She walked around defeated,
professing that love from others was never needed.
All she had was herself,
so, she would be all right,
yet she carried that burden
for more than half of her life,
blinded to the fact that she was broken.
She was unsure of how to get free,
so, she unleashed her pain on everybody.

Physically all seemed well,
but mentally
emotionally,
she was in hell
and no one could tell,
because early on she was taught how to keep secrets.

4 A.M. QUESTIONS

Sometimes, I wonder if my husband is alive.
Was he aborted because religion, family, and socioeconomic status deterred his mother from carrying the promise of God's son?
Was she raped, or did she just produce with the wrong guy, deciding that it was easier to kill him than live with the shame of her mistake? Did poverty result in him being born too soon, not ready to live outside of the womb?
So, if he was born,
was his masculinity robbed at the hands of a trusted male figure?
Is it that life was too much for him and he found comfort in a bottle?
Or did the needle, pipe, white line, gambling, or quest to get money make everything seem fine?

Is he in jail because the fast life seemed easier than getting his education or starting his own business?
Did envy, emotions or danger cause him to sin against his brother, son, cousin, or father?
Was he too "black"?
Did he fit America's perception of a little, ghetto boy or did they fear him because of the skin he was born in?
Did he have his life taken away from him by the hands of an international terrorist, or more sadly a domestic one, clothed in blue, white, or black?
Is he full of pride? Does he secretly hate women because his mother never showed him the love he needed, simply because she was too busy chasing men who abused of her physically and emotionally?
Is he so insecure that he works too much, putting on the façade that he has it going on through his love of expensive cars and clothes?
Does he believe what the media says about me,

THE SOUL OF A BLACK WOMAN

that I am beneath him, a whore and its too
many of us to settle down with just one?
Is he intimidated by my strength because of the
power struggle inflicted since slavery?
Or is he attached to the wrong woman, who kills
his dreams, emasculating every desire he has
because he is so turned on by her idolized image
of a bad chick, failing to see that the cost of her
bags, surgical enhancements,
red bottoms, 24"inch weave,
and Hollywood girl status was robbing him
blind.
There is an all-out war against our brothers and
because of the struggle,
I'm sitting here praying for you
The battle is so thick,
that you don't even know what to do.
Wake up Black men,
some of us do still want you.

SPIRITUAL WARFARE

Sometimes, I wish that you could understand
how hard I fight for you.
I fight so hard that my stamina fails,
because I'm constantly taking jabs from you.
I cry out, but you don't seem to hear it.
Then I get frustrated
because I waited so long for you to notice,
and you didn't.
Sometimes, I shed tears because it's easier to weep.
You compliment everyone else on earth,
but you find so much fault in me.
I am subjected to your every emotion,
but you downplay my existence.
When you get weak,
I be screaming "Don't trip because I know we can fix this!"
Sometimes, I wonder do you love me?

THE SOUL OF A BLACK WOMAN

Do you value me?
But you're too busy to get that deep in relationship with me.
I go to God asking him to show me how to reach you.
Honestly, I don't know what else to do.
We try so hard to teach too,
providing solutions and intuition,
but you rely so heavily on the world
that you ignore what the Word has already given.
Sometimes, I wish that you would stop allowing them to validate you.
Beloved you were made perfect because God created you.
Stop, look, pray, and listen.
God assigned us to you.
Sincerely, Jesus and the Holy Spirit.

ALONE

Alone.
I go into this dark world, alone
Trying to give light to those along the way.
If only I pretend to fit in,
just maybe they will notice me.
The smile that I flaunt is deceiving,
as no one really knows the burdens
held captive in my mind and heart.
I appear unmoved
as the bitter winds of life blow,
destabilizing the foundation that I used to know.
Somewhere in between the coming of age
and the realization that a woman has arrived,
I lost a part of me,
questioning everything.
I recall being a young girl
who couldn't wait to become a woman.

THE SOUL OF A BLACK WOMAN

I listened to the anthems that said I was a
woman,
Now hear me roar,
rehearsing the lines in my mind
of how I could be and do anything.
But wow,
did life sure make a fool of me.
I worked hard to get an education,
Meaning I didn't really have time to date,
spending long hours at the job
trying to keep busy,
because no one seems to understand me.
I sit in the office
overhearing the conversations
of who is doing what this weekend
with whom.
Then when I am asked what my plans are
I get creative
Making up lies to make my life seem busy as
theirs.
I go to bars with friends,
empty

but it beats going home
to be alone.
I avoid friends and family
just so they won't be asking whether I have a
man
or in some cases a woman because they think I
have some sort of secret life,
when will I have kids,
why do I work so hard?
when was the last time I went on a date?
and what happened to the guy that I bought
over three years ago?
Then in the next instance,
because I don't have either,
I am always volunteered to do for others,
simply because people believe that I have no
other responsibilities.
Because of the education
and the little money that they assume I have,
I am expected to give to everyone else.
With men,
I am too independent, or I want too much,

Because I don't want to have to take care of someone.
Some days
I just want to be appreciated and cared for too.
After this prayer,
and after I dry these lonely tears,
I guess I will whip up this hair,
Apply this makeup,
And look in the mirror to see if this outfit looks right.
I will tell myself,
"It's gone be a good day, girl, you got this",
Readjusting this mask
so that I can appear to the world
as if I am so full of life
and cool with being alone.

REAL LIFE

Growing up was supposed to be simple,

especially if you're walking in the purpose that was meant for you.

Oh, I miss the days of my youth

Speaking about the woman I was becoming

Excited about the things that I would do.

But I was unaware of the challenges brewing

I thought that I knew what I was doing.

But reality hit me,

and I learned real quick that life was a bully.

Nobody told me that I would have to endure

the highs, the lows,

the yeses and the nos.

But there's no surprise

even in frustration, I still gotta wipe my eyes

and perform.

A CONVERSATION WITH (DIFFERENT) GODS

Me:
Lord, I am tired of being alone
on the real,
God, I'm sick of doing it all on my own.
God, I grow tired of being told to just stay strong.
Tell me why I gotta hold on to this so long?
EVERY woman in the world has someone but me?
God show me exactly what I'm NOT doing?

God:
My child, I know what I promised you,
plus, I know your heart,
because I created every intricate part.
Just trust me daughter.

Me:

Ok, God, I mean, I guess I understand,
but your sons never chose me,
I done tried to be the woman
you said I should be.
I'm starting to believe that no one wants the gift
of me.
Now God,
I done wrote down what I wanted
and prayed for what I think I needed,
but still I just haven't received it.

God:
Beloved, remember, I've known you since you
were in the womb,
I have a plan for you,
stop moving so soon.
Girl, can you please just let me complete the
work in you?

Me:
But God, you're taking too long!!

Satan:
Girl, you know that God ain't real.
If he was,

he would have given you what you wanted,
right?
He does say that he's a jealous God.
He only wants you to himself.
You like them tall,
right?
A family man?
You love them medium to dark chocolate,
right?
Oh, and because you are so independent
he gotta have a job,
making that plant money.
He must dress well,
Rocking them beards, smelling good,
and drive them big body trucks you like.
He gotta have some swag too.
See I told you,
I know what you like.
Since your "God" ain't listening,
let me do you one better,
I got one just for you.
You just wait and see Boo.

God, Jesus, and the Holy Spirit:
Well y'all,
she does have the freedom to choose.
Well, we already know,
Give her some time to heal
Because herself and her faith,
she's about to lose.
She's venturing into dark places.

THE SOUL OF A BLACK WOMAN

PART II:

DARK PLACES

The light shines on in the darkness and the darkness did not understand it or overpower it or appropriate it or absorb it [and is unreceptive to it].

"In life, we all have valley and peak moments. Each stage is needed to sustain and prepare us for our own individual greatness. Those moments are testimonies that are not intended just for your benefit, but to guide and help someone else during their valley or peak moment."

Meika J Cole

JOURNEY PRAYER #3

God, I messed up, AGAIN. Lord, are you punishing me for my mistakes, known and unknown? Relationships should NOT be this problematic. God, am I not good enough? Did I do too much or not enough? God, why did I feel the need to deceive my mate the way I did? God, why did I lose my parent? Why didn't I get the job? Lord, why did my friend betray my trust? Why did I lose my child? Father your word says:

"The Lord is near to the heartbroken And He saves those who are crushed in spirit (contrite in heart, truly sorry for their sin). Many hardships *and* perplexing circumstances confront the righteous, But the Lord rescues him from them all.

He keeps all his bones; Not one of them is broken."
Psalms 34:18-20 AMP

Well, God help me. Father heal me, hear my cry Lord. Please restore my broken places so that I can be made whole again. Lord, I know these tears are cleansing me. God, I am so sorry for letting you down.

In Jesus Name, Amen.

Dark places? Now why would I want to expose anyone to my dark places? I mean, I've lived through them long enough, so why should I revisit them? We often think about what would happen if people got a chance to see our flaws. To what extent would they judge us? Who would they tell? That is when we allow the Spirit to lead us because like the old saying goes, "everything ain't for everybody."

In life, we all have valley and peak moments. Each stage is needed to sustain and prepare us for our own individual greatness. Those moments are testimonies that are not intended just for your benefit, but to guide and help someone else during their valley or peak moment. See, the thing about these places is that someone, somewhere, may be on the verge of giving up and your dark place moment may just be what motivates them to regain their strength and confidence.

Dark places allow us to be barren. Akin to a desolate alley, it stinks, and you don't know what may be lurking around the corner. I don't know about you, but for me, I did some dumb stuff in those places. Because light didn't dwell there, I allowed myself to be blind. In some areas, you feel so lonely that you are unaware of the spirits that you invite in. You feel stuck and don't know how you will break free. You invite brokenness, insecurity, guilt, and depression into your essence.

I have come to the supposition that for us to recognize and value the light, at some point in our lives, we must withstand being in the dark. In the dark places, you learn who you are. If you don't know what does and does not work for you, how can you get free?

The one lesson that I learned, from being in that place, was that God does hear us and loves us anyhow; but the enemy will, in fact, try to keep you bounded to that place. The Word says:

If we [freely] admit that we have sinned *and* confess our sins, He is faithful and just [true to His own nature and promises], and will forgive our sins and cleanse us *continually* from all unrighteousness [our wrongdoing, everything not in conformity with His will and purpose]
I John 1:9

I recall speaking with a woman who admitted to having relations with a married man, while I don't condone it, she felt that she would always be punished because of that one transgression. I assured her that if she asked God to forgive her, with her whole heart and to pledge to never do it again, she would be forgiven. If He forgives her, He would do the same for you. Don't let your dark places abort the plan that God has for you. Where you fall short, ask that He give you strength.

THE SOUL OF A BLACK WOMAN

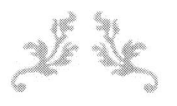

HEART REALITIES

I will admit,
I messed up
I gave in too quick
well, because
I wanted you.
I went in heart first,
but somewhere along the way,
I lost your attention
as I caught feelings.
I wanted it,
but you didn't
Bae, I've noticed the distance,
daily texts
have become less and less.
The let me hit you backs
are becoming more frequent.
You've been throwing hints,

I haven't missed it,
I just was hoping it was not what you meant.
I must show you my loyalty,
try hard to make you believe,
that there's no one better than me.
I believe that you can and will change,
so, I tell myself that I must wait.
I gotta continue encouraging you
If your heart is what I want to pursue,
right?

TO HAVE AND TO HOLD

I took your last name
in hopes of being happy forever,
but if this is your definition of forever
I don't know if I want it.
Some days I stop loving you,
Because I feel like you stopped loving me
a long time ago.
It's like you got me,
but you forgot that marriage must be
maintained.
I need you to remind me
that I am just as beautiful today
as I was back then,
but you don't.
You expect me to be your everything
but when I need you,
you think that I am nagging you.

MEIKA J COLE

When I come to you,
you're too busy,
Too sleepy.
I feel alone
not just right now
but all the time.
To have and to hold, huh?
To death do us part?
That is what we said.
I just hope that we can get it right before then.

LYING TO MYSELF

Yo' check it,
I would appreciate
if you respected
my stance.
I'm sure that you think I need a man,
ff course, I want it
but I want stability too,
cuz' simply put,
I refuse to be used.
I don't want a man treating me
any kind of way
just to say that
I have somebody,
but honestly
I am lonely.
I got a friend or two,
who may fall through,
but they ain't saying nothing

that I want to hear.
So out of fear,
I keep them close,
just in case I get lonely.
A relationship?
Nahh, I don't need all that
cuz' these dudes out here,
They super wack.
They ain't faithful,
so why should I be?
I'm gone play the game
before they play me.
But in all actuality,
this ain't what I want.
So, I will continue to talk
all big and bad
but when I'm done talking
I will still be sad.

I CHEATED

Heaviness was evident in my countenance
As I battled the thoughts in my head.
Should I go or should I stay,
those were the words that I constantly said.
I tried to justify
the lie that I was so good at telling myself.
Acting more like the villain,
instead of being my husband's help.
I stood before God,
proclaiming vows
to love this man for life,
Now I am blaming him
because I didn't know my role as his wife.
Questioning if he loves me,
instead of looking at his actions.
I failed to acknowledge all that he did,
because I was in my own world
thinking about what he could do for me,

instead of focusing in on we.

Constant arguing,

and nights sleeping apart.

It was just the start

of my indiscretions.

Thinking that the grass was greener,

cuz' ole boy's game looked a little bit meaner.

Blind to the fact that

what I had at home was a winner,

but there is no way I can correct it,

In one moment, I messed up my forever

for one minute.

It hurts like hell to admit,

I failed my family,

when I cheated.

ENROUTE THOUGHTS

And she thinks to herself...

1st Hour En Route: I wish this car would speed up. Like seriously fool, the speed limit is 70. I gotta get to my baby so I can get checked into this hotel before 6. I don't know why I keep doing this. I done worked all week and now I'm spending 4 hours one freaking way, driving through these sticks. I better slow down cuz' them troopers be deep out here.

2nd Hour En Route: Why can't I kick Mr. Smith? When he was out, his tail didn't even act like he had time for me, now he blowin' up my phone every couple of hours, sending letters and hand drawn cards and junk talking 'bout he love and miss me. Sending Jpays asking for some money. Saying he's sorry and he wants to be there for me. He wasn't saying all that when he was getting Kee-Kee pregnant, and getting shot at by Michelle's dude, all while still being married to Trina. Every time he in need, he calls me. Like that time when Vanessa tried to put that baby on him, and when Peaches slashed his tires. Oh, but let's not forget when the Narcs raided his momma house. Where were those females at then? He was calling me.

3rd Hour En Route: I don't even got kids by this dude. All we got is history. I've loved this dude harder and longer than any man I've ever encountered, but he has never chosen me, and here I am still holding on to the what ifs and the maybes. But on the other hand, he knows I got him. I'm gon' show him that I got his best interest at heart. I been giving him scriptures and praying for him, so he knows I'm a God-fearing woman. He gon' be so pumped, cuz I been talking to his momma and she finally gave me the recipe for that lasagna he like with the polish sausage in it. Eventually, he gon' see that I'm the prize. I got a good job, I'm educated, ain't got a bunch of babies running all around, I pay my own bills, and I ain't laying up with everybody. I'm loyal and he knows that I'm down.

At the entrance: I bet he gon' be looking sexy, cuz' on them last pics he was buff then a mug. Hello Sir. Wait, what do you mean he has a visitor already?

Trina Smith, are you serious??!!

WHAT YOU DOING GIRL?

Friday 3:30 p.m.
What you doing girl?
Yes, I got it all planned out.
When I leave this job today,
it's all about bae no doubt.
It's been a minute and we both been busy.
I know he miss me
cuz' he been texting me like,
"What's up Sexy".
Girl, I'm bout send him a text back saying, "Why
don't you fall through?"
So, soon as I get home diva,
I'm gone call you.

7:30 p.m.
What you doing girl?
My bad, I had to make a couple of stops.
I got some chicken and veggies in the oven,

hold on, let me set this clock.

He loves to eat

so, I step up my game.

I want to show him not all independent women

think the same.

I'm submissive.

Girl what?

Did I buy some wine?

Heck no,

he likes Hennessy with cranberry

and a splash of lime.

That's wifey material right there, boo.

My table is already set up too.

Yes girl. He gone be over about nine,

and my mission is to blow his ENTIRE mind.

I got them mahogany teakwood candles that he likes,

yes, that's gone set the mood off just right.

Honey, I forgot to tell you,

I been on that diet.

I am so glad that you told me to try it.

Paired with them two months in the gym, my

glutes and abs looking real tight.

No, girl I got me a sew in,

cuz' he told me that he hates the natural look again.

Remember that set I told you I got from the Secret?

Do you think those red bottom heels gone look right with it?

All right cool,

let me get myself together,

and later on,

I'm gone call you.

11:15 p.m.

What you doing girl?

Oh no, he ain't got here yet.

I was calling to see

if you could fit me in tomorrow for a full set?

Ok cool.

Oh snap, this is him calling right now,

So, in the morning,

I'm gone call you.

Saturday 10:30 A.M

What you doing girl?

I'm feeling kinda blue,

do you believe this Joker called,

but never came through.

Well, right now

I'm in my feelings boo,

so later on,

I'm gone call you.

LOST DREAMS

As far as she could recall,
the thought of you was always with her.
She prepared for you since she was four or
maybe it was three,
regardless of the age, she knew just what kind of
mother she would be.
Like her momma, she would feed you,
love you,
making sure that you were always protected
never feeling rejected,
and would make sure that you were always
respected.
Somewhere between the peak of womanhood,
she got scared,
cuz' momma let her know, off the rip, what
would happen if she came home pregnant.
So, she waited,
but love was young, and passions were burning,

young and dumb, she surely gave in.
She conceived accidentally,
two times,
but her body couldn't quite sustain the life
that was growing inside.
After the miscarriages,
She learned to stay protected,
and she chased after her dreams,
but in the back of her mind she still longed to be
a mommy.
In the meantime, she had given up on the
possibility of ever carrying you.
But God spoke to her in a dream saying, surely,
she would conceive.
10 years to the day, she got the news that she
was carrying you.
She and your dad was surprised
because they couldn't wait to meet you!
For five whole months,
they were in awe too.
She had so many plans for you.
She figured that she would paint your room

THE SOUL OF A BLACK WOMAN

blue,
and since you finally emerged,
maybe she would be able to have another child
or two.
Again her body gave in,
She was told that you were trying to break
through.
Even after being stitched up,
Two weeks later,
you decided that the womb was not comfortable
enough.
Enroute to the hospital,
she was ready to meet you,
but 5 months was way too early for you.
She prayed,
and cried,
she told the doctors that their assumptions were
lies.
She tried to encourage everyone that you would
be alive.
She felt you moving on the inside,
fighting hard for your life.

But they said you were too small
your lungs weren't developed,
therefore you couldn't survive.
You were coming,
and there was nothing she could do,
She felt like less of a woman,
because already,
she had failed you.
She cried and pushed,
Pushed and cried,
all while praying to God that you would be alive.
at 6:18 a.m. she gave birth to you,
You took one final breath
as she held on tight to you.

BABY MOMMA

Suffice it to say,
she didn't imagine her life this way.
When she gave herself to you,
she expected to grow old with you,
cuz' that's what expectant parents do.
While her upbringing wasn't perfect,
she knew having both parents in the home
was worth it,
because it was all she knew,
she couldn't help but expect to be living that
same life too.
She thought that you would make her your wife,
especially since you talked about how you
needed her in your life,
Heck, she was playing the role already,
right?
But she was deceived,
while carrying your seeds

twice.
Because you showed her early,
that you wasn't about that life.
Maybe she was a fool
for constantly laying with you,
but it's what her heart and soul
was connected to,
simply because she saw something in you,
that maybe you didn't even see within
yourself!
She thought that she would receive your
protection
instead, all she got was your rejection
Such a harsh lesson to learn
carrying a child that you reminded her
time and time again
that you never wanted.
She went to prenatal appointments alone.
Nursing herself when she was sick at home.
No baby get me some pickles and ice cream
or requests to rub her swollen feet
because he wasn't there

to meet her needs.
No pregnancy pictures for her
because it was not an image she enjoyed.
She toyed with the idea
that maybe when the baby came
you would change,
but what she learned
was that the relationship with you
would never be the same.
What she learned was how to make due
because she really couldn't rely on you.
Now while you are out making new families
arguing that she is jealous of your newfound
happiness,
just know that your baby momma
and child are doing fine without you.

SIDE CHICK CONFESSIONS

Indeed,
I see the fury and hatred in your eyes
and I apologize
but it is what it is.
I wish I could offer a remedy,
for the hurt that you felt because of me.
I get it
He cheated
you can't forget it
But you forgave him.
So, miss me with the evil looks
and side eyes,
because I am trying to pick up
the remnants of my life,
because he never told me
that he had a wife.

THE SOUL OF A BLACK WOMAN

While he was away with you,
doing what a "family man" supposed to,
I believed the lies about working overtime
so that he could provide for his kids.
I was playing my position,
Not to mention,
trying to downplay
that female intuition,
because real talk,
my spirit wasn't really with it.
something just didn't feel right,
but I didn't want to be that woman
constantly assuming,
cuz' I didn't want to ruin
the pseudo-reality
of him and me.
Yes, I will admit,
there were inconsistencies
but because of my relationship history
I chalked it up
cuz' I thought I was thinking too much.
Eventually,

I let my flesh get the best of me
because I loved our chemistry.
So, I totally overlooked the discrepancies
in all of his stories
believing him when he said he loved me.
See, we had more than just a fling,
things were mental
later morphing into the physical.
My Father wasn't pleased
so, he removed my blinders
and let me see some things.
That's when the streets told me about you,
and eventually you found out about me too.
But, what you didn't know was that a child was
conceived.
So, to protect myself
I terminated my seed.
Living daily with shame,
because that was not the life I saw for me.
Daily I struggle with the fact that
I dishonored myself
and I disobeyed God.

THE SOUL OF A BLACK WOMAN

You chose to stay,
While I decided to pray.
Asking God to forgive me
for my indiscretions,
learning from painful lessons
of the heart.
And I pray that all is well with you
But Sista girl,
you gone have to stop
mean mugging
when you see me out.
I understand that you were hurt
I was deceived too
So, the next time you see me
understand that this hurt I have
Goes far deeper than you.

DEAR (INSERT NAME)

Dear (insert name),

    I wish I had the opportunity to tell you how I really feel. Since you've been gone, adjusting to life has been hard. In the back of my mind, I wanted to spend forever with you but realistically, I knew that would never happen because of her. I will be honest, as naive as this may seem, I still had hope that maybe something would happen, and you would see just how much I loved you with my whole heart. Yes, I played a fool and I held that title for far too long.

Dear (Insert Name),

    I gave you my loyalty, and I shared with you my dreams. I let you in (insert name). As foolish as it seems, I still let you in. Into my emotions, my present, my fears, my strengths and into my spirit. My soul mourns secretly, because although I want to hate you, I still love you. The fact is, there was always her, and I question if everything you said was real. I question if I was just another notch on the belt. Did you love me like you said you did? So now what do I do? Huh? Do I try to move on knowing that it hurts like hell? Do I accept the fact that you chose her over me? Do I need to continue to act like it doesn't bother me, although I hurt so bad?

No, I just gotta keep living, but in all, I thank you for the life lesson. I'm bitter as hell, but eventually I will forgive you. But most importantly, I will forgive myself. But it will never ever happen again. Thank you (insert name) for planting the seed.

FRIEND ZONE

She is...
Faithful
Reliable
Inspirational
Encouraging
Not one to lie to you
Discerning
Zealous
Open-hearted
Noble
Enduring...

Yet, as beautiful as she is, you keep her in the friend zone. You tell her your secrets, wants, and desires. She celebrates you and prays hard for you. But, you are so focused on the one who doesn't have your best interest at heart, that you overlook her every time.

SCARED

I'm so far removed from the possibility of being
in love because I'm scared.
Scared that I may get it wrong again,
falling for someone who doesn't see me more
than just a friend.
Scared into thinking
that I may not measure up,
because the stereotype is that women like me
aren't easy to deal with.
I long to spend my nights sitting on the phone
discussing your day.
I want to laugh and make plans for the
weekend.
I want flowers sent to my job.
I want him to spend time getting to know me
like I would with him.
Because I dreamed that he would do just that.

MEIKA J COLE

I know that I am worth it
but do I deserve it?
I don't know.

JOURNEY PRAYER #4

Jehovah God, I come to you, asking that you forgive me. Lord, please assist me where I fall short. God, allow me to stop trying to live my life without you in it. When I do things outside of your will, I make a mess of my life. I find myself in places that I don't belong. I end up hurt, feeling less than, and questioning my worth. I compare myself to others and downplay the beauty that you placed in me. God, your word states:

"The LORD is near to the heartbroken and he saves those who are crushed in spirit (contrite in heart, truly sorry for their sin)."

Psalms 34:18 AMP

God, I am asking for you to understand my heart. Help those whom I've hurt to find forgiveness in their hearts for my sins against them. Most importantly, give me the tools that I need to forgive myself. Lord, I ask that you cover my children, allowing them to never have to experience the darkness that I have. God, I pray for better days. I pray that you will release me back to the light, so that I may have life and have it more abundantly.

In Jesus name, Amen.

THE SOUL OF A BLACK WOMAN

PART III: WELCOME BACK TO THE LIGHT

Pleasant words are like a honeycomb,
Sweet *and* delightful to the soul and healing the body

Proverbs 16:24 AMP

"Detach yourself from the noise, so that you can learn to listen again."

Meika J Cole

As I reflect on the numerous stories that I have told and those that has been shared with me, I have finally concluded that in order for us as Black women to be who God called us to be, we have to get to the place of moving beyond our past. Life happens in seasons. Yes, I know that those dark places shaped us, but God did not intend for us to be held captive there for the rest of our days. All that I can say is don't be like Lot's Wife. If you recall the story at Genesis 19, here were the distinct instructions from the Father:

"When morning dawned, the angels urged Lot [to hurry], saying, "Get up! Take your wife and two daughters who are here [and go], or you will be swept away in the punishment of the city." But Lot hesitated *and* lingered. The men took hold of his hand and the hand of his wife and the hands of his two daughters,

because the LORD was merciful to him [for Abraham's sake]; and they brought him out, and left him outside the city [with his family]. When they had brought them outside, one [of the angels] said, "Escape for your life! Do not look behind you, or stop anywhere in the entire valley; escape to the mountains [of Moab], or you will be consumed and swept away."
Genesis 19:15-17 AMP

As you can see the directions were very clear, but Lot's wife had an issue—she was content with the way things were, unaware of the goodness that God had awaiting her. She liked her life as it was, and she was good. The word goes on to say:

"But Lot's wife, from behind him, [foolishly, longingly] looked [back toward Sodom in an act of disobedience], and she became a pillar

of salt."
Genesis 26 AMP

So now my question to you is, what are you telling yourself and how many of you are pillars of salt because you keep flirting with your past? Why do you continue to entertain thoughts and actions that keep you bound to dark places? Why are you still trying to fit into molds that weren't created for you in the first place?

With every offense, disappointment, and "woe is me" moment that I had ever experienced, I eventually came to the point of either giving up or giving in. I had believed that I couldn't be loved. I told myself that I was barren and would never bear children. I didn't think I would get to a place of pure happiness. I told myself that God would never forgive me for my indiscretions. It was that very thinking and speaking that made my light dim. It kept my life noisy with all the things that were so not of God. Eventually, you must detach yourself from the noise so that you can learn to hear again.

With listening comes clarity. In order to know who you are and to understand the promises of God, you must first seek His counsel, read His word, and take time to learn just who you are. You must get to the place of knowing your worth, but you can't successfully do this without going through some rough patches.

Once you realize the power that you were born with, those dark places won't even matter. When your soul is settled, you can be open to love, mend a relationship, and let go of the guilt and regret. Start living again. Become optimistic, and in time, your light will shine so bright that others will want to know what you did. It's an easy answer—You became one with the spirit. Now it's your time to encourage someone else.

JOURNEY PRAYER #5

Jehovah Heavenly Father, thank you for every journey and testimony that you allowed me to overcome. I declare that my sad days are behind me because you gave me the tools that I needed to get past them. Lord, thank you for reminding me of my worth, my purpose, and the real reason you why created me. You made me to be the head and not the tail. Because of your love, I am renewed and ready to live my best days. God, I know the road will never be perfect, but long as I know that your direction is perfect, I am content.

God, I thank you for allowing me to see my faults. I humbly accept your correction. God, thank you for getting me past the pain. Lord, thank you for preserving my heart. I thank you for allowing me to be made whole again. Lord, I anticipate the good that is now coming my way because I gave you back the wheel. God, your word says:

Delight yourself in the LORD, And He will give you the desires *and* petitions of your heart.

Psalms 37:4 AMP

Jehovah God, I am ready. I am now in the position to hear you and gain all that is destined for me. Thank you for healing my relationships. Thank you for building each of us up, one step at a time. Lord, thank you for allowing me to be used as a vessel for someone else who felt the way I did.

In Jesus name,
Amen

FREEDOM

You know,
I never really took the time to see
that sunshine greets me daily,
reminding me,
that I have purpose.
It took some time to learn this
as tragedy made me focus.
See,
I was so hung up on what did and didn't work,
I had dreams
which I never birthed,
because I was too scared to push.
Push beyond the pain,
I was content with that place,
I felt like I had nothing to gain.
Then life made me take a second look.
Death has me shook.

I've said goodbye to people
who begged for one more day to be alive,
Apologizing and asking God for a second
chance at life.
Yet, I stay anchored to the past.

But today,
God gave me my discharge papers
I am no longer bound to my past.

HEY, DID I EVER APOLOGIZE?

I must admit, I was caught up in who I thought would protect the delicate nature of me, so I overlooked you.

I disregarded the genuine "Hello, how you doings" and the many "You look beautifuls" because I was attracted to a weaker version of you.

Your strength was not recognized at the time, because Mr. Right gave me a distorted sense of security. I was allured by his smile, not seeing deception unraveling slowly but surely. He made me feel alive as I competed for his attention, not to mention the loving that I was getting had me mesmerized. So, gone to the point that I failed to identify the lies and pseudo portrayals of love that my heart constantly justified. So, now I'm asking you, Did I Ever Apologize?

    Because you weren't rocking the latest threads, Jordan's or Timbs, I felt that you were beneath me. Being with you wasn't my destiny, because I was too busy looking at the eye candy. Eventually, all of that "candy" made me sick, and I lost all the confidence that I had in me. I almost killed myself trying to be the woman that he wanted me to be.

    So, when he decided that the other chick could offer more than me, I was left devastated, ready to unleash my anger on any man that would ever try to court me. Even in that, you still noticed me, but I didn't acknowledge that you were there willing to give me all the love that I could ever need.

    So now, again, I am asking,
    Did I EVER apologize?
Through my subtle rejections, I made you

question the connection that you had with me. I helped you to harden your heart, now you are doing other women the same way that Mr. Wrong did me. Guess it's all a circle of our history and now I'm telling you
I'm sorry....

I AM THE PRIZE

Really, I'm not insecure
I'm just unsure
of what you want me to be.
I lost a bit of myself
when you said you loved her
but not me.
I got too much pride to let you see
the pain forming internally,
So I played it off casually
but my heart was broken.
In that instance,
I knew that I couldn't compete
you let me know right then and there
that I was in a race alone,
even though my feelings were strong.
I took the lesson as another love casualty,
because in friend zone is where you placed me.

THE SOUL OF A BLACK WOMAN

So I admit I cry
Even though I try
to remember the strength that I have within.
That's when I realized
on the real,
I Am the prize
and now I can stop living my life
as your option.

REVELATIONS

I was waiting too long apparently,
Because the revelations were in front of me.
God removed my blinders so that I could see,
That tribulations made the best of me.
No longer living my life second guessing,
Stressing,
Crying over spilled milk
taking more pills
in hopes of correcting my health.
I had to learn thyself
and be content with me.
No more comparing myself
to jaded images on the TV,
cuz' I realized the power that resides in me.
Now I can see that I'm truly free
because of the things that were revealed to me
I was waiting too long apparently,

because the revelations were in front of me.
God removed my blinders so that I could see,
That these tribulations made the best of me.

KINDA LOVE

I want to experience agape love.
unfiltered
compassionate,
putting everything on the line for each other
Kinda Love.
I want that sitting in the car,
listening to 90's R&B,
with red cups,
reminiscing about jeans with the leather on the front, debating which was the coldest,
Cross Colors or Used Jeans Kinda Love.
I want that planning the menu for our Super Bowl,
chilling with our friends,
trash talking over Uno and Spades
finishing each other's sentences,
watching Love Jones and X-Men,

THE SOUL OF A BLACK WOMAN

falling to sleeping on the couch together
Kinda Love.
I want the Kinda Love that accepts me
despite those few added pounds I gained,
the newfound grey hairs,
and monthly emotional outbursts.
I want the Kinda Love that allows me to feel
secure in being who God made me to be at all
times.
I want our kids to see God in our union,
no focusing on who does what,
when,
but working collectively,
making sure that it's a win-win
for everyone involved Kinda Love.
I want the Kinda Love that allows me to
encourage you
without you feeling as though
I'm trying to change you.
I want the Kinda Love that is felt not only by
us,

but one that our true friends and family pray that we have.
I want the Kinda Love that has no reservation in giving.
I want the Kinda love that will give me peace when my world feels like a lonely place.
I want the Kinda Love that never gets stale.
I want to do random stuff.
Not too extraordinary,
but that simple kinda love.
Yes, I want that hanging out,
laughing,
having drinks at a hole in the wall on Saturday night,
followed by wing dings and fries from the Coney Island,
waking up Sunday morning for church together Kinda Love.
I want to the Kinda Love that gives me 100% confidence in your ability to lead us,
as God and Jesus leads you.

THE SOUL OF A BLACK WOMAN

I want the Kinda Love spent in the car at night,
under the stars,
talking about our expectations of God,
and praying together that He orders our steps.
I want the Kinda love
that wants this Kinda love too.

A BETTER VIEW OF HIM

Last Night,
the Father showed me a glimpse of you.
I saw the promise and blessing
and it was so beautiful.
You saw the very depth of me,
your spirit was open
and you knew just what I needed.
For once, I was in the presence of a whole man,
who so dearly wanted to be by my side.
You saw the broken pieces of me
that I tried to hide within the fragile
compartments of my heart.
You saw my strength and weaknesses,
but you said that you wanted it all or nothing.
You wanted to show the world
the love that you had for me.
Providing me with what my heart

truly deserved.

You showed me that you could care for me

and our babies.

Giving me full security in the realization of us.

You assured me of the possibilities

God told you exactly what my life was missing.

I felt heaven's promise when I dreamed of you,

now I must open my heart

and be ready to receive you.

JUST ONE TIME

Just one time..
I want to experience love
With a receptive heart
Not consumed with the what ifs
of him potentially hurting me.
I don't want to be constantly looking for the
warning signs of his infidelity,
or keeping an account of the lies that he forgot
he told me.
Just one time...
I want to be confident knowing that he has the
best intentions for me,
and that he trusts me to protect his dreams.
I want to be bold in declaring the love I have
for him,
making our love the greatest story ever told
Just one time..

THE SOUL OF A BLACK WOMAN

I want to experience butterflies every time he's
near me,
giving into his every desire,
reciprocating the same chemistry
he gives to me.
Just one time...
I want to get it right.

WORTHY

I'm not perfect
nor do I profess to be,
but I am glad
I now realize
that I am truly worthy.
I am worthy of every blessing that's due to me,
I just need to be patient
and see
the grace and favor over my life,
flowing so abundantly.
I don't have to worry about
who accepts
or rejects me,
cuz' I got the revelation
that I am a gem
and God said I was worthy.

RENEWED

My love, when I'm with you
feelings of desolation escapes me
because you truly make me happy.
I'm renewed.
I walk close to you
trying to focus in on your heartbeat,
listening to see if our rhythms are in sync.
When I look to you, I see past your faults,
because I see the promise in you.
Whenever I'm around you I feel free,
engrossed in new opportunities
and experiences.
I see greatness,
and I feel your energy.
So I inhale you,
making sure that the fullness
never escapes.
Suffice it to say,

MEIKA J COLE

I pray that it stays this way,
because I now know what love, freedom, and
peace feels like,
because God manifested it through you.
My love, I am so happy that we fell in love again.

ALL IS WELL

After all was said and done,
My spirit had finally danced.
When I wiped my eyes,
a sense of pride filled me up on the inside.
It overpowered every bad circumstance,
rejection, and disappointment.
In that moment,
I felt like a little girl
because my innocence was restored,
and I didn't have a care in the world.
I finally got my spirit realigned.
I am so glad that my Father spared my life.
No longer in darkness,
because now I am better able to produce in the light.
Again, all was well with my soul.

FOR LAILA

In a little while,
you will soon understand the sacrifices,
nights on the computer
pumping papers
to present at scholarly conferences.
I'm sorry I had to say no when you wanted to
play,
but I always promised that one day
we would be ok.
I try so hard to keep you secure
even if I'm unsure in the process.
I stand before you, giving you all of me,
rising above everything
that was meant to break you and me.
You are the reason that I strive harder.
Through your love and God,
I was able to hold on longer.
Statistically, I should be certified crazy

But your strength is the very thing that saved me, from me.

THE END

ABOUT THE AUTHOR

Meika J. Cole is a mother, daughter, sister, and friend first; activist and critical cultural scholar second. Born and raised in Pontiac, Michigan, Meika's love for writing, speaking, and her aspiration to get involved in the lives of Black women led her on an enriching road to spiritual discovery.

Meika attended Oakland University in Rochester, MI, where she obtained a Bachelor of Arts and Master of Arts degree in communication, with emphasis on critical cultural communication.

Meika lives in Auburn Hills, Michigan with her daughter. She is currently pursuing a doctorate degree in educational leadership and is working on her second book release, *Broken Woman: A 30-Day Devotional to Overcome Spiritual Brokenness,* to be released Summer 2018.

For more information about the author and upcoming releases, please follow Meika using the social media channels below:

Social Media Contacts
Website: www.meikajcole.com
Blog: www.soulofablackwoman.com
Facebook: www.facebook.com/meikajcole/
Instagram: www.instagram.com/j_meika/
Twitter: www.twitter.com/j_meika